Pocahontas
C.S. Woolley

Level 3

900 Headwords

Pocahontas
C.S. Woolley

First published 2017
by Foxton Books
London, UK

Copyright © Foxton Books, 2017

ISBN: 978-1-911481-06-5

Interior and cover illustrations by Stefano Popovski

Cover design by Alexander Solovyov

Foxton Readers are a series of carefully graded books aimed at ESL / EAL learners of beginner to advanced levels. They are based on a comprehensive grammar and vocabulary framework to match each ability level and to ensure each learner progresses. They are not only suitable for ESL / EAL learners but can also be used with native speakers of primary school age.

Printed and bound in Turkey by Onka Printing Ltd.
Printing press certificate number: 20419

CONTENTS

INTRODUCTION

There are many legends and stories about Pocahontas. She was the daughter of the chief of her tribe. Because she was the daughter of the chief, the English called her a princess. She made friends with the white men and even fell in love.

Pocahontas was a real person although there are some things in the legends that were made up. There are other things we do not know and have to guess.

The story of Pocahontas is about other people too. Her father, Powhatan, Captain Smith, the Governor Sir Thomas, Captain Argyll and John Rolfe. This story looks at all the facts that were written down by the people who met Pocahontas and her people. It is the real story of the Indian Princess, not a fairytale.

ABOUT THE AUTHOR

C.S. Woolley (Caroline Sarah Woolley) was born in Macclesfield, Cheshire and raised in the nearby town of Wilmslow. From an early age, she discovered she had a flair and passion for writing. This was fuelled by winning local poetry and short story competitions during her years at Mottram St. Andrews Primary School.

During high school, she continued to write. She began writing novels at the age of 14. University did nothing to change her love of writing. C.S. spent a year reading Law at Manchester Metropolitan University before changing her mind and moving to read English at Hull University. After graduating, she moved to Nottingham where she lives now.

CHAPTER 1

Pocahontas was a clever and pretty girl. Her father was called Powhatan.

He had many names and titles. His people sometimes called him Ottaniack, sometimes Mamauatonick, and Wahunsenasawk.

He was chief because he was born to the chief. He had more land than his father because he had won wars. The chiefs of other lands had lost their land to him. Others called him a friend so he did not fight them.

He had several camps. He lived in different ones at different times. Wherever he lived, he was with all his wives and a guard of **bowmen**. When he was bored with a wife, he gave her to his favourite warriors. Then he would choose a new wife from the beautiful, young girls of the Indian tribes.

All his people obeyed him with fear and love. They gave him anything he wanted when he asked for it. His people brought him gifts and were scared if he was unhappy.

He gave **harsh** punishments to those who broke the law. His warriors beat some people to death in front of him. They tied some to trees and cut them up like meat, joint by joint. They **broiled** others to death on burning coals.

bowman (n) a person who shoots with arrows, an archer
harsh (adj) not kind or gentle, cruel, severe, difficult
broil (v) to cook something (especially meat) under direct heat

They tied some to trees and cut them up like meat,
joint by joint.

Now I will tell you what the Indian people looked like and how they acted. Powhatan's people had their own religion. It wasn't like Christianity. They had priests that did magic. They didn't have churches. They had houses that they used for their faith.

They kept lots of drawings in the houses and did their magic in them. They didn't pray to their gods to help them but to stop evil. They didn't believe in heaven or hell.

Captain Smith wrote about one of their magic spells. In this spell, they killed some of their children for their gods. Parson Whittaker, who calls the Indians "naked slaves of the devil," also says, "They killed adults and children for their gods."

Parson Whittaker sent a picture of their god to England. He said, "Their priests are like our English **witches**. They call them Quockosoughs."

The men of Jamestown believed that the Indian priests were like witches and that they controlled the weather.

The Indians had red skin that made them different from the white men of Jamestown. The first Englishmen to go to Virginia all thought that the Indians were born with white skin. Then their skin turned red because they put red cream on it. They thought the cream was made from roots and dirt. The white men thought that the Indians used the cream to stop mosquito bites.

The Indians loved pretty things like earrings and necklaces.

witch (n) a woman with magical powers

They had priests that did magic. They did not have
churches. They had houses that they used for their faith.

CHAPTER 2

In 1608, when she was 12 years old, she met a man called Captain Smith.

The white men had come across the sea to Virginia from England with their governor, Sir Thomas Dale. They fought with Powhatan's people. Powhatan's people caught Captain Smith. They put him in prison.

Pocahontas saved Captain Smith's life. The white men liked Pocahontas.

Powhatan told Pocahontas, "Go and see Captain Smith. Many of our people are their prisoners. Ask Captain Smith to let them go."

Pocahontas went to the white men. She went to talk to Captain Smith. She spoke to him and he let the Indians go as the sun set. Pocahontas and Captain Smith fell in love. When he was a prisoner, he fell in love with Pocahontas. In 1608, Captain Smith married Pocahontas.

Captain Smith wrote about Pocahontas in the letters that he sent back to England.

In 1608, she met a man called Captain Smith.

It was usual for Indian girls to get married when they were very young. Powhatan, Pocahontas' father, had lots of wives. He had twelve favourite wives, twenty sons and ten daughters.

There are other people who wrote about Pocahontas too. William Strachey, who was a 17th century English writer, wrote about Pocahontas in his book, but his words about her are the same as the words Captain Smith wrote. People **argue** about who copied who. It looks like William Strachey copied from Captain Smith.

William Strachey didn't see Pocahontas when he was in Virginia. She didn't visit the camp after Captain Smith left for England in September 1609.

Pocahontas didn't get any letters from Captain Smith after he left. She began to think he was dead.

According to William Strachey, Pocahontas married again. He wrote that she was married to an Indian called Kocoum after Captain Smith left, but this may be wrong as we know that Pocahontas married John Rolfe in 1614.

Captain Argall was the captain of a ship that England sent to Virginia. He arrived in Virginia in September 1612. He planned to kidnap Pocahontas so that he could free the white slaves that Powhatan had.

Captain Argall was a bold man, who always did his duty, **no matter what**.

argue (v) to discuss something with someone who thinks differently from you
no matter what (phrase) regardless of the consequences

Japazeus, King of Pasptancy, helped Captain Argall to trick Pocahontas.

Captain Argall also wanted to get back the tools the Indians had stolen and get some corn for the colony.

She went on to Argall's ship. The white men caught her.

In April 1613, the white men took Pocahontas prisoner. The Governor, Sir Thomas Dale told the white men, "Go and capture Pocahontas."

It is hard to know how old Pocahontas was at this time. Her father didn't keep records. She was probably 18 when the white men took her.

Pocahontas was a gentle and fair girl. She liked the white men in Virginia because of Captain Smith.

She was like other Indian girls before the white men took her. She was the daughter of the chief but that did not make her special. It was the English who called her a princess.

She didn't act like a princess when she was "cart-wheeling" about the **fort**.

Between 1609, when Captain Smith left, and 1613, when the white men held her prisoner, we don't know what happened to Pocahontas. The Indians didn't write books about her.

fort (n) a strong building (generally soldiers live there)

She went on to Argall's ship. The white men caught her.

Argall sent a message to Powhatan. He said, "We'll let Pocahontas go if Powhatan does what we want."

Powhatan agreed but the men didn't let her go. Powhatan sent home some of the white slaves, one broadaxe, a long whipsaw, and a canoe of corn, but Pocahontas had to stay in Jamestown.

In March 1614, Sir Thomas Dale and Captain Argall went to see Powhatan. They took Pocahontas with them. They asked, "Will you fight or will you give back the things you stole? When you give back the stolen things, Pocahontas can come home."

Two of Powhatan's sons wanted to see their sister. When they saw that she was well, they went to see their father. They told him that they could make peace with the white men.

John Rolfe went to talk to Powhatan but it was his brother, Apachamo, the next man to be chief, who made a promise for peace.

While Pocahontas was a prisoner, she fell in love with John Rolfe and John Rolfe fell in love with her.

The Governor said to John Rolfe, "You can marry her."

In April 1614, John Rolfe and Pocahontas got married and their marriage brought peace between the Indians and the colony.

John Rolfe was a hardworking man. He had a daughter called Bermuda but she was not Pocahontas' daughter.

John Rolfe worked hard for the colony and was the first man to try and grow tobacco for it.

Nobody knows how Pocahontas passed her time while she was a prisoner. She could not do what she did in her father's camp. Many people think that she had lessons from Sir Thomas Dale. He taught her to speak English. She learned how the white men lived. John Rolfe and Reverend Whittaker also taught Pocahontas about God.

In April 1614, John Rolfe and Pocahontas got married.

CHAPTER 3

Sir Thomas Dale was a very good governor. The town was lucky to have him.

In 1609, he did a very good thing. He changed the law. At that time, the law said that the people of the town could not own land. Sir Thomas changed it so that they could. This made things better for the town right away. It made the white men better people.

When they first came to Virginia, they were not nice people. They were **rough** men.

People in England said that Virginia was not a good place to visit. "Virginia is a bad place, a nest of rascals, loose women, cads and evil people. It is a place of painful work, bad habits and poor diet."

Governor Dale was a soldier and wanted to see the colony improve. He was sure that the Indians would become Christians.

When John Rolfe and Pocahontas had married, she had been a Christian. This success made Governor Dale decide to try and convert Pocahontas' sister. He sent Ralph Hamor, his secretary and Thomas Savage, a boy that the Indians knew to talk to them. They went to ask if the Governor could have another one of Powhatan's daughters.

rough (adj) unpleasant, violent, not careful, not kind

18

Powhatan greeted Ralph and Thomas when they arrived. He hadn't seen Thomas for four years. The two talked about what had happened. Then they went into Powhatan's hut to talk. Powhatan's servants offered them a pipe of tobacco, which Powhatan first smoke, and then passed to Ralph Hamor.

Powhatan greeted Ralph and Thomas when they arrived.

Powhatan asked how Sir Thomas Dale was, then he asked about Pocahontas and her marriage to John Rolfe. Ralph told him that his brother and his daughter were well. Pocahontas didn't want to come back and live with him. Powhatan laughed and said, "I'm very glad about that."

Then they began to talk. First there was a message of friendship from the Governor. Powhatan got presents of coffee, beads, combs, fish hooks, and knives, and a grindstone.

Then Ralph asked about Powhatan's youngest daughter. Powhatan replied with pride to the message of friendship and promised his people would keep the peace Pocahontas' marriage had brought.

His youngest daughter was not there. Powhatan said that he had sold her to be the wife of another man and she had left three days before.

Ralph didn't give up. He said that the marriage was not a problem. Powhatan could call his daughter back because she wasn't old enough to marry.

The Governor said he wanted to pay three times the price of Powhatan's daughter in beads, copper, **hatchets**, and many other things.

Powhatan said he loved his daughter as much as his life. He had many children, but he loved her more than the others. He said that he had to see his daughter every day.

Powhatan didn't want to sell his youngest daughter to the white men.

hatchet (n) a small axe

20

Powhatan said, "I don't need any more signs of friendship from the Governor. I gave Pocahontas to the white men as a gift. When she dies, I will send a new child as a present to Jamestown."

He added, "It's not very nice of the king to try and take two of my children at the same time. Please tell him I am his friend. I won't hurt his people or start a fight. My people won't hurt his people or fight them. Many people have died. I won't let more die in such silly fighting as long as I am chief. I am old and I have spent most of my life fighting. I want to live in peace. I don't want to fight and then die. My people will leave instead of fighting. We will go far away as my country is very big."

Ralph and Thomas stayed with Powhatan for two days. They came back to Jamestown with a present for John Rolfe and Pocahontas. Powhatan asked for his son and daughter to send a present to him. He told Ralph and Thomas to give a message to the Governor,

Powhatan said, "I hope this makes the king happy. I will move three days away from here if the king is unhappy and I will not see any more Englishmen."

Not long after this, in 1616, Governor Dale left Virginia and did not come back. He returned to England with John Rolfe, Pocahontas, and several other Indians. When he left, there were some problems that led to a **mutiny**.

mutiny (n) rebellion, uprising, not obeying orders and causing trouble

At Plymouth, Tomocomo got a long stick and began to
make notches in it for the people he saw.

Tomocomo, the husband of one of Pocahontas' sisters, and an advisor to her father came with her on a **pilgrimage**.

The ship waited in Plymouth though England was not a good place for the Indians that came with Pocahontas.

Many of them became sick and died not long after they arrived. Another became a fortune-teller in Cheapside. Two of the Indian girls went on a ship to Bermuda to try and find husbands.

Tomocomo had many conversations with important men in London. He educated them about his people and his land. He showed them how they danced and how the spirits had taught him to ride horses. They all thought he was a **savage**.

Powhatan had asked Tomocomo to take a census of the people in England and tell him what they were like. At Plymouth, Tomocomo got a long stick and began to make notches in it for the people he saw. He soon gave up because there were so many people.

pilgrimage (n) a journey to a holy place
savage (n) a cruel and violent person

CHAPTER 4

Captain John Smith heard that Pocahontas was arriving in England. He hadn't seen her since he left Virginia.

Captain Smith wrote a letter to Queen Anne. He asked her to speak to King James about Pocahontas. He did this because Pocahontas was a princess. You can see the letter he wrote in his book *General Historie*.

The letter reads:

"To Queen Anne of Great Britain

Most well-liked Queen

The love I have for God, my King and country has made me go to the most dangerous places. Telling you the truth in this letter, your Majesty, is the most dangerous thing. I know that I might look ungrateful by writing this letter. I am sorry. I want to thank you for all that you have done for me but I must tell you of what is happening to Pocahontas.

Ten years ago, when I was in Virignia, the Indians caught me. Powhatan was their king and a very powerful man but they did not treat me badly. They were good to me.

The people who were the nicest to me were Pocahontas and her brother, Nantaquaus. Nantaquaus was a very strong and bold man. He was the best man of his people.

Pocahontas was the favourite child of the chief. She was 13 but very kind to everyone. She did not like fighting. She wanted peace. That's why I liked her.

I was the first white man and Christian to meet Chief Powhatan and his people. They were scary men and my enemies but they did not hurt me. They only bullied me with their words.

I was in the Indian camp for six weeks. I was their enemy and the chief said they would kill me because I was his enemy.

They tied me to a stone and the chief had his stick ready to kill me but Pocahontas stopped him. Pocahontas put her head between my head and the stick. She saved my life.

Then she asked her father to send me back to Jamestown. The chief sent me back to the camp with a guard. I was safe. At Jamestown, I found the 38 men were all sick. They did not have any food and were weak. Pocahontas saved me again. She came with food so we did not die. We all survived thanks to her help.

Powhatan was not happy that Pocahontas helped us so he told her to stop coming but she did not listen. She came to Jamestown at night to see me. She was not scared of the dark or travelling through the frightening woods.

We talked a lot. She told me what to do to not make her father angry. For two years, the men of Jamestown did not die because Pocahontas gave us food.

When I left Virginia, the Indians and men of Jamestown started fighting. Nobody saw Pocahontas for two years.

Your people made peace with the Indians and Pocahontas came back. She met John Rolfe and married him. She left behind the faith of her people and became a Christian.

She came to England with her husband and is here now. She is the first one of her people to speak English. She has a son with John Rolfe. She is the first of the Indians to have a child with an Englishman.

They tied me to a stone and the chief had his stick ready
to kill me but Pocahontas stopped him.

27

*Most kind Lady, I have told your Majesty about Pocahontas. I have told you the truth. I know that there are better people to tell you about Pocahontas. But I have not lied to you. I have never asked for anything from my country. I know I am not a **worthy** man and that John Rolfe is not important enough to come and visit you.*

Pocahontas is a princess that left her own kingdom to be part of yours. She gave up being a queen to live in England. If we don't treat her well, she might change her mind about Christianity and peace with England.

She might be angry. She might hate England and make lots of problems, but if the Queen of England asked her to visit and was nice to her, it would make her happy. I am not telling you what to do but ask that you think about it. I am your servant and simply kiss your kind hands."

When Pocahontas got to England, Captain Smith was getting ready to go away on his ship for the third time.

Pocahontas wasn't staying in London. She was in a place called Branford. She was there because there was too much smoke in London. Captain Smith went to visit her in Branford. When he went to see her, Pocahontas was angry with him. She thought he was dead because he did not write to her.

worthy (adj) good, of high quality

Tomocomo was with Pocahontas. He told Captain Smith that Powhatan had told him to find Smith. He asked that Captain Smith show him his God, and the King, Queen, and Prince.

When Pocahontas first got to England, she met the King, Queen and Prince.

CHAPTER 5

When Pocahontas arrived in London, there were many people who were interested in seeing her. She saw the King and Queen and met with many important people but after that we don't know very much about her.

Many people in England were interested in knowing about Indians. Because Pocahontas was a princess, people wanted to know even more about her.

She went to the English court. She talked to Dr. King, the Bishop of London.

When they acted Ben Jonson's *Christmas his Mask* at court, in January 1617, Pocahontas and Tomocomo were both there. Chamberlain wrote about their visit.

"The Virginian woman, Pocahontas and her father's man met with the King. They liked Ben Jonson's play. When she came back, she looked sad, like the wind was about to take her away."

She saw the King and Queen and met with many important people.

Rich people ignored Pocahontas. They were more interested in John Rolfe's loyalty.

Peter Fontaine wrote, "When they heard that Rolfe had married Pocahontas, people talked about high **treason**. People thought marrying an enemy princess was treason."

treason (n) the crime of helping the enemy of one's country, especially during a war

Pocahontas had different names. Her people sometimes called her Matoaka. She became a Christian and had a Christian name, Rebecca.

Pocahontas or Lady Rebecca died on a ship. It was at Gravesend when she died. She had been sick for three days.

The doctors said, "It's smallpox" but we don't know much about the cause of her death. They buried her at St George's Church. A fire destroyed the church in 1727.

Pocahontas never returned to see her father.

John Rolfe became Secretary of Virginia and Captain Argall became Governor, but people did not like him because of his bad nature.

In August 1618, the people of the Virginia Company wrote to Captain Argall, "We do not know why you told us that Opechankano and his people want Thomas Rolfe to be in charge. I think you are trying to use it to make you more important."

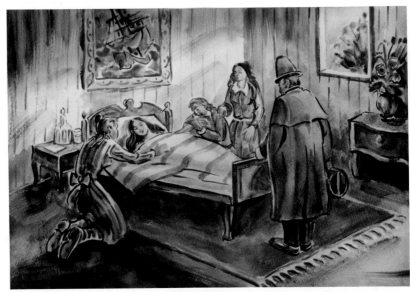

Pocahontas or Lady Rebecca died on a ship.

John Rolfe died in Virginia in 1622. He had a few children when he died. He married a new lady after Pocahontas died. No one knows the name of his third wife or when they got married. John's brother, Henry Rolfe, looked after Pocahontas' and John's son after John died.

Their son was called Thomas Rolfe. When Pocahontas died, he went to live with Sir Lewis Stukely of Plymouth. He wasn't a good man and Thomas had to move. This is how he came to live with his uncle, Henry Rolfe. Henry Rolfe made sure that Thomas went to school in London.

When he was grown up, Thomas went to Virginia. In 1641, he asked the King, "Can I go and visit my aunt Cleopatra?"

He had to ask if it was okay to go and see her because she was an Indian. Cleopatra was the sister of Pocahontas and lived in the Indian lands. Men had to get permission to go and visit the Indian lands.

Thomas had one daughter. She married Colonel John Bolling. They had a son, Major John Bolling. John Bolling named his son after himself and he also had five daughters, all of whom married. They married Colonel Richard Randolph, Colonel John Fleming, Doctor William Gay, Mr. Thomas Eldridge and Mr. James Murray.

In 1618, Powhatan died. He had enjoyed his life of fighting and living in his land.

Powhatan is a very important man in early Virginia history and he deserves his place. He was a clever man. He did a good job stopping the white men from stealing his land but he was not as clever as Captain Smith.

There is something sad about the end of his life. He was very upset that Pocahontas had died so far from home and in a strange land. There were lots of white men who came to Virginia and stole the land from his people.

He had asked for peace and said he would move away from them. He only wanted the white men to leave him and his people alone.

CHAPTER 6

Pocahontas was a rare woman. She was very brave and kind. Her Indian people were **cruel** and nasty, but Pocahontas was not. She was a hero with a heart that did not use fighting to solve problems.

There is not one writer who says anything bad about her. They all say good things about Pocahontas. She had a gentle nature.

As a child, she acted like other Indian children but she found the white men interesting. This changed her from an Indian girl into a legend.

cruel (adj) not kind or gentle, violent

Her heart made her like the white men. She worked hard to help them and save them. Pocahontas became the first friend to the white men in Jamestown. She became friends with the white men very quickly. She was a very good learner. She became a Christian because she loved the white men who told her about God.

The fairytale story of Pocahontas says that she did more than save the life of Captain Smith. The wish to save the men was normal to a Highland girl or an African maid. Pocahontas saved a man who came to take the land of the Indians for England.

Pocahontas did everything she could to make peace with the white men. Even when the white men did not act like they wanted peace, Pocahontas still helped them.

The white men were cruel to the Indian people. When they were **running out** of food, they made the Indians give them more.

The Indians didn't have enough food to feed their people and the white men. When they said no, the white men did horrible things to them.

The white men burned down the houses of the Indian people and shot some of them.

run out (phrasal verb) if you run out of something, you use it up, you finish it

The white men burned down the houses of the Indian people and shot some of them.

Pocahontas knew what the white men were doing to her people. She still helped them. When the Indians were going to attack the white men, Pocahontas informed them. She **let down** her own people to help the white men.

She liked living with the white men. She learned how to act like an English woman. She learned to speak English. She married an Englishman and had a little boy. She chose the white men over the Indians.

let down (phrasal verb) to disappoint

There is no writing that tells us what her people thought about Pocahontas. The white men did not write down anything about her.

People remember Pocahontas as a young and beautiful woman. She didn't live long enough to learn about the nasty side of the English.

She didn't see how men used the Christian faith that she loved for bad. She didn't see her husband as a bad man or see him fail.

Pocahontas didn't see the attack on Jamestown in 1622. Powhatan was dead and Opechancanough was chief. Opechancanough didn't want peace. He attacked Jamestown. An Indian boy told the white men about the attack but Opechancanough still killed 347 people, men, women and children. There were only about 1388 people living in Jamestown.

THE END

Opechancanough did not want peace.
He attacked Jamestown.

GLOSSARY

argue (v) to discuss something with someone who thinks differently from you

broil (v) to cook something (especially meat) under direct heat

bowman (n) a person who shoots with arrows, an archer

cruel (adj) not kind or gentle, violent

fort (n) a strong building (generally soldiers live there)

harsh (adj) not kind or gentle, cruel, severe, difficult

hatchet (n) a small axe

let down (phrasal verb) to disappoint

mutiny (n) rebellion, uprising, not obeying orders and causing trouble

no matter what (phrase) regardless of the consequences

pilgrimage (n) a journey to a holy place

rough (adj) unpleasant, violent, not careful, not kind

run out (phrasal verb) if you run out of something, you use it up, you finish it

savage (n) a cruel and violent person

treason (n) the crime of helping the enemy of one's country, especially during a war

witch (n) a woman with magical powers

worthy (adj) good, of high quality

ACTIVITIES

COMPREHENSION CHECK

Test-1

Are the following sentences True (T) or False (F)?

1. The white men never fought with Powhatan's people. T / F

2. Powhatan never trusted his daughter. T / F

3. While Pocahontas was a prisoner, she fell in love with John Rolfe. T / F

4. Powhatan had twelve wives. T / F

5. Pocahontas didn't like the white men. T / F

6. Captain Smith wrote a letter about Pocahontas to King James. T / F

7. Powhatan loved his youngest daughter so much. T / F

8. Pocahontas saved Captain Smith's life. T / F

9. Captain Argall was a nice person. T / F

10. Pocahontas disappointed her own people to help the white men. T / F

11. People in England were not interested in knowing about Indians. T / F

12. Indians kept lots of drawings in their houses and did their magic. T / F

Test-2

Match the sentences.

Beginnings

1. The white men had come

2. Pocahontas was a princess

3. Indian girls got married

4. The men of Jamestown believed

5. The Indians had red skin

6. When Pocahontas arrived in London,

7. John Rolfe married a new lady

8. Pocahontas became a Christian

9. Powhatan was very upset

10. When Captain John Smith heard about Pocahontas arriving in England,

Endings

a. and had a Christian name.

b. across the sea from England.

c. that made them different from the white men of Jamestown.

d. who saved Captain Smith's life.

e. he wrote to Queen Anne about her.

f. there were many people who were interested in her.

g. when they were very young.

h. after Pocahontas died.

i. that Pocahontas had died so far from home.

j. that the Indian priests were like witches.

Test-3

Who said this in the story?

Sir Thomas Dale, Captain Argall, Powhatan,
Captain John Smith, Thomas Rolfe or Parson Whittaker

1. "Go and capture Pocahontas."

    ....

2. "We'll let Pocahontas go if Powhatan does
    what we want."

    ....

3. "When she dies, I'll send a new child as a present to
    Jamestown."

    ....

4. "Ten years ago, when I was in Virignia, the Indians
    caught me."

    ....

5. "Can I go and visit my aunt Cleopatra?"

    ....

6. "They killed adults and children for their gods."

    ....

7. "It is not very nice of the King to try and take two of my
    children at the same time."

    ....

GRAMMAR CHECK

Test-1

Circle the correct form of the verbs in italics.

Example: I didn't understand what he *was asking* / *is asking* for.

1. Powhatan was not happy that Pocahontas *helped* / *helps* the white men.

2. The chief said they *would kill* / *will kill* me because I was his enemy.

3. Powhatan said that he *had to see* / *has to see* his daughter every day.

4. He was sure that the Indians *would become* / *will become* Christians.

5. Nobody knows what Pocahontas *did* / *does* when the white men took her.

6. When they first *came* / *come* to Virginia, they were not nice people.

7. When Pocahontas got to England, Captain Smith *has got* / *was getting* ready to go away on his ship for the third time.

8. John Rolfe *marries* / *married* a new lady after Pocahontas died.

9. Pocahontas knew what the white men *were doing* / *are doing* to her people.

10. When Pocahontas *died* / *dies*, her son went to live with Sir Lewis Stukely of Plymouth.

Test-2

Choose the best answer.

Powhatan is a very important man in early Virginian history and he ¹ .... his place. He was a clever and sly man, and he did a good job stopping the white men from ² ....
his land, but he was not as clever as Captain Smith. There is something sad ³ .... the end of his life. He was very upset ⁴ .... Pocahontas had died so far from home and in a strange land. There were many white men ⁵ .... came to Virginia and stole the land from his people.

1.   a. deserve   b. derserving   c. deserves
2.   a. stealing   b. steal   c. to steal
3.   a. for   b. about   c. on
4.   a. which   b. where   c. that
5.   a. what   b. who   c. when

Two of Powhatan's sons wanted ⁶ .... their sister.
When they saw how well she ⁷ ...., they went to see their father so they could ⁸ .... peace with the white men. John Rolfe went to talk to Powhatan but it was his brother, Apachamo, the next man to be chief, ⁹ ....
made a promise for peace.

6.   a. to see   b. seeing   c. see
7.   a. is   b. was   c. has
8.   a. do   b. get   c. make
9.   a. which   b. who   c. when

Test-3

Put these words in the correct order so that the sentences make sense.

1. hard / colony / the / John Rolfe / worked / for

....

2. lucky / town / him / the / was / to / have

....

3. them / many / of / became / and/ sick / died

....

4. chief / child / the / Pocahontas / the / was / favourite / of

....

5. head / my / between / Pocahontas / put / stick / her / head / and / the

....

6. her / with / husband / England / Pocahontas / came / to

....

7. learner / was / Pocahontas / a / very / good

....

8. her / anything / write / about / down / the / white / men / did / not

....

VOCABULARY CHECK

Test-1

Choose the best answer

1. She fiercely .... with her husband last week and she hasn't talked to him since then.

   a) argued   b) cared   c) lied

2. We won the battle and .... hundreds of enemy soldiers.

   a) greeted   b) copied   c) captured

3. They .... me at the door and gave me a very warm welcome.

   a) shook   b) greeted   c) lost

4. Pocahontas was a woman with a .... nature. She was kind to people.

   a) gentle   b) rough   c) cruel

5. He doesn't like animals and he is .... to them.

   a) soft   b) cruel   c) nice

6. Eating food high in fat .... to obesity.

   a) makes   b) leads   c) rescues

7. Only three passengers .... the accident. The rest died.

   a) survived   b) confused   c) built

8. She .... all of her friends by not coming to the party. They all wanted her to come.

   a) amused   b) disappointed   c) entertained

9. Our charity did a lot for .... causes last year. For example, we organised fundraising events for the homeless.

   a) worthy   b) painful   c) evil

10. Every year, millions of Muslims go on a .... to Mecca

    a) mutiny   b) cause   c) pilgrimage

Test-2

Choose the best answer

Pocahontas knew what the white men were doing to her people. She [1] .... helped the white men. When the Indians were going to [2] .... the white men, Pocahontas informed them. She [3] .... down her own people to help the white men.

1.	a. and	b. still	c. then
2.	a. greet	b. return	c. attack
3.	a. let	b. met	c. treated

Powhatan [4] .... Ralph and Thomas when they arrived. He had not seen Thomas for four years. The two talked about what had [5] .... Then they went into Powhatan's hut to talk. Powhatan's servants [6] .... them a pipe of tobacco, which Powhatan smoked first and then passed to Ralph Hamor.

4.	a. greeted	b. survived	c. copied
5.	a. amused	b. happened	c. died
6.	a. ate	b. tricked	c. offered

ANSWER KEY

COMPREHENSION CHECK

Test 1

1. False
2. False
3. True
4. True
5. False
6. False
7. True
8. True
9. False
10. True
11. False
12. True

Test 2

1. b
2. d
3. g
4. j
5. c
6. f
7. h
8. a
9. i
10. e

Test 3

1. Sir Thomas Dale
2. Captain Argall
3. Powhatan
4. Captain John Smith
5. Thomas Rolfe
6. Parson Whittaker
7. Powhatan

GRAMMAR CHECK

Test 1

1. helped
2. would kill
3. had to
4. would become
5. did
6. came
7. was getting
8. married
9. were doing
10. died

Test 2

1. c
2. a
3. b
4. c
5. b
6. a
7. b
8. c
9. b

Test 3

1. John Rolfe worked hard for the colony
2. The town was lucky to have him.
3. Many of them became sick and died.
4. Pocahontas was the favourite child of the chief.
5. Pocahontas put her head between my head and the stick.
6. Pocahontas came to England with her husband.
7. Pocahontas was a very good learner.
8. The white men did not write down anything about her.

VOCABULARY CHECK

Test 1

1. a
2. c
3. b
4. a
5. b
6. b
7. a
8. b
9. a
10. c

Test 2

1. b
2. c
3. a
4. a
5. b
6. c